Weaving the Boundary

Volume 79

Sun Tracks
An American Indian Literary Series

Weaving the Boundary

KARENNE WOOD

TUCSON

The University of Arizona Press
www.uapress.arizona.edu

Printed in the United States of America
21 20 19 18 17 16 6 5 4 3 2 1

ISBN-13: 978-0-8165-3257-5 (paper)

Cover designed by Leigh McDonald
Cover image: *Weaving Water 13* by Sarah Sense

Publication of this book is made possible in part by the proceeds of a permanent endowment created with the assistance of a Challenge Grant from the National Endowment for the Humanities, a federal agency.

Library of Congress Cataloging-in-Publication Data
Names: Wood, Karenne, 1960– author.
Title: Weaving the boundary / Karenne Wood.
Other titles: Sun tracks ; 79.
Description: Tucson : The University of Arizona Press, 2016. | Series: Sun tracks: an American Indian literary series; 79
Identifiers: LCCN 2015029046 | ISBN 9780816532575 (pbk. : alk. paper)
Subjects: LCSH: Indians of North America—Poetry. | Indians of North America—History—Poetry. | Indians of North America—Social conditions—Poetry. | LCGFT: Poetry.
Classification: LCC PS3623.O63 A6 2016 | DDC 811/.6—dc23 LC record available at http://lccn.loc.gov/2015029046

♾ This paper meets the requirements of ANSI/NISO Z39.48-1992 (Permanence of Paper).

For from what could we weave the boundary

Between within and without, light and abyss,

If not from ourselves . . .

—Czesław Miłosz

CONTENTS

Weaving the Boundary

PART I

TO KEEP FAITH

Homeland

Inaugural poem, National Council of the
Lewis & Clark Bicentennial, 2003

Blue mountains encircle a prayer
to the mist we call breath of the dead—
everywhere, seeds lie dormant
in the ground. This is a country
remembered—dogwoods, redbuds,

deer at field's edge, the river roiled
into its embrace of red earth. We are
powerless here, in the face of our
love for legends of granite
and shapes that gather at night.

We are powerless when
mountain laurel spreads its stars
through forests, when cedars
dance with the yellow leaves falling,
and hawks cry out over us.

Shadows move west, then east,
a circle of two hundred years.

On the Missouri, a man with braided hair
tells himself stories and looks at the sky.
He guards sacred places of his people,
a hundred miles of shoreline, and he is alone
when he faces the ones who would steal
from those graves, robbing the spirits.
He is made from the dust of their bones.

A Montana woman wrestles barbed wire
and drought, searching the skyline for rain.
Her grandfather plowed this same ground.
So she goes into it, freckled and burned
by the beauty of pastures where calves graze,
lavender mountains rising to the west,
the vanishing outlines of wolves at twilight.

And in Lapwai, the Nez Perce leader
holds his hand out to the future
where forgiveness lies within himself.
He remembers years of winter
and the chiefs who would not leave.
His prayer heals a generation—
a red flower's fingers, uncurling.

Nothing was discovered.
Everything was already loved.

To Keep Faith

It's an idea like light, the star's trajectory
over sacred places that rise from their landscapes:
dark mesa, dark desert tower, dark river swelling
across the shadowed fields of the republic.

This is your passion: to save the earth's cathedrals.
The machinery of our country's interests works
against it. In another city, you might have disappeared,
blindfolded at sunrise with hands behind your back.

In another time, not that long ago, I might have
found you face up in a field of silence among the still-
beautiful bodies of Dakota men. To speak
for the earth: I say history is against us here,

as though you hadn't already recalled who I was
before I learned to be wary of stories or as though
your words hadn't entered me like light,
small wavecaps riding on all that darkness.

For you, then, some words about light. Relentless
light. Incantatory words we could lick like
blue flames. Words to keep faith with each other
and earth, that searing love, which still claims us.

The Egg

The nest of grass and hair slapped with mud
teeters above one window's left shutter.
A phoebe built it three weeks ago, as she did
last year. On the glass table under the nest,
a tiny shattered egg.
                    Opaline, not even an inch long,
glued to the glass with a bit of dried albumen,
the shell's curvature reveals a folded embryo,
dried up, its oversized head resembling any other
embryo—reptile, mammal, bird—but smaller
and in profile, one purple-black eye unseeing.

Embryo, whose root means "to swell, or be full"—
in this case, shrunken. Gamete, zygote, mitochondria.
Neurogenesis. The hapless cells, dividing. And then.
In this case, potential hatchling, unhatched. It never
breathed. I scrape the shell's remnant from glass
and set it under the hydrangea.
                    Uninhabited,
its spirit has already diffused into everything.

The continuous incarnation.

Seeds

Sunstruck, they suspend themselves
from tendril, twig, or tip—
a dazzling array of devious designs
to propel plants' pollinated progeny—

parachutes, pinheads, pods of all stripes,
hitchhikers, husks, helicopters,
thistle-puffs, potato tubers, peach stones,
avocados' gorgeous globes, wheat grains,

rhizomes, strawberries' sequined
epaulets. Eaten and ejected,
forgotten by forest foragers, diffused—
few find their difficult way.

Some are watertight. Some retain
hulls until heated or humid enough. Some,
like jack pine and cypress, pop open
after a fearsome fire, for regeneration.

They dangle, drop, float, drift, and glide.
Look: the air above the lake is alive!
In moldering loam, limp leaves unfurl
and thrust themselves into the light.

Dancing the Stars

You dance the grasses as grass shifts to shadow,
arc of stars' silver points cast across the black waters, each
sinuous blade blazing like lightning at night. You are
a flute of wind that stirs the field and leaves it changed.

You dance red-streaked fire, eyes searching mountain
forests, until there is only fire, only primal heart,
blood, claws, bared teeth, a lone warrior backlit in flame—
that story of battles, hunts, steps of celebration.

You dance air through which the sky's monarchs
dart together, fanfare of sunset, one singular flower
emblazoned on a field and vital as the sun. You are
a luminescent shawl of light returning our vision at dawn.

And you dance the river, banks dressed in snow, sun
rising behind black bare trees—that slow grace of water,
which flows and flows on and yet remains the same,
its current sweeping always toward the ocean.

Each of you, dancing your journey of stars—this is where
the body pulses around the earth's heartbeat, rhythms
aligned within an ancestral circle, where those whose hearts
dance themselves become the drum that goes on.

The Point

In autumn we crept down a mulched path
to the bank where cattails shone, bulrushes
concealing scarlet flags of the blackbirds.

The forest: humid scent of leaf-mold,
skittering of squirrels, the old buck's track
toward a copse of knotted cedars.

I wanted to believe it wouldn't end
and stepped behind you soundlessly
like one of the spirits who inhabit

these woods. We reached the blind,
finally, and trained our field glasses
until a few white spots gleamed—

eagles' heads against pines—there, on the ridge.
Then, above us, one rose, and I held my breath.
There's a furious sound—seven feet of wing

feathers displacing the air. What remains
as it ascends but a repetitious longing
and the silence that follows departure?

Wind for days, and then frost. As I walked
the trail without you, my shoes crushed
a lace of ice. Every eagle was gone.

Once I held one in my sights until its shape
blurred—the horizon overtook it, and the haze.
I scanned but could not locate the vanishing point.

A'nó:wara

for Powhatan Red Cloud-Owen

He was born at Akwesasne, between New York and Canada.
On his father's side, Mohawk—the Kanien'kehá:ka, People
of Flint, who call the earth A'nowara ko:wa, Turtle Island.
His family, Turtle Clan. His mother, Chickahominy—their symbol,
the turtle. In 1955, the St. Lawrence Seaway project relocated
his family and flooded their home. After high school in Virginia,
among his mother's people, he married his sweetheart.
Got drafted. Went back to Akwesasne for a ceremony—
four young Mohawk men, going to war. To Chu Lai, Vietnam.
Americal Division, Dottie LZ, 1968, after Tet. Three months
of humid heat, AK-47s, Otis Redding's "Dock of the Bay" every
night, mortars exploding, playing cards, looking for land mines
and Charlie. Choppers overhead—Chinooks brought soldiers in,
took wounded out, Hueys dropped guys to recon, brought most
back. A routine patrol. Lifting out, at tree line, their chopper
took a direct hit and exploded, killing those in front; rear prop
still spinning, the Huey spiraled, crashed, splashed fuel, and
spat men out the side door in flames. He ran right at the
enemy, his chest on fire, screaming, till his buddy rode him down.
He'd go home with his side lacerated, second- and third-degree
burns over more than a third of his body. He was twenty years old.
Months of recovery. Years of rage. No one notified his family,
welcomed him home, taught him how to survive after war, how
those three months had changed him—you take nothing with you
when you die, but what do you carry when you live? Friends who
didn't make it. Nightmares. Scars. At Akwesasne, another ceremony,
one used to heal warriors for hundreds of years. All four had returned.
No word in any language can describe what had happened to them.
In Washington, Americans call the Vietnam Memorial "The Wall."
He sees himself reflected in polished black granite: igneous rock,
formed beneath the earth by liquid fire. Through his own image,
he reads names of those who died and sees their faces in his own.

A Vietnamese woman speaks to him, thanks him for his service,
says her country is grateful. In 1968 she had not yet been born.
She asks about his turtle medallion. Her people call the Great Turtle
cu rùa, a term of respect. It symbolizes heaven, earth, and long life.
He withdraws a beaded turtle pin from his pocket, its colors those of the
American flag. As he hands her the gift, something inside him uncoils.
It can take forty years to know what home is, and how to get there.

Boundary

for my father

I travel alone, as though gathering medicine:
moose and elk on Trail Ridge,
bighorn in the Badlands,

Anasazi ruins at Bandelier. I map America
as homage to you. Somewhere
between Canyon de Chelly

and Bear Butte, I forgave myself for being
unable to save you. Each effort a fractal.
Love: absolute and impotent.

Black wings, spirits, ice. Across the estuary,
a glacier's core shudders. It calves. The sea
heaves. I know the way back

like crosshatched, stained trails on hands
of those men who lowered
you into the ground.

Triolet for the Road

So, claim it. Peer through the cracked windshield. These losses.
Garbage, roadkill. We keep going. There is nothing to do.
At least as much of a curse as the old mariner's albatross is,
clamoring, appearing through the cracked windshield, some losses
haunt me. Drunk wrecks between Tucson and the rez. Highway crosses
litter Route 86 as though handfuls of conquistadors came through
and claimed it all. What appears through a cracked windshield? Losses,
garbage, roadkill. Keep going. There's nothing else to do.

Red Elk

in memory of Daniel Red Elk Gear,
April 2014

I.

We found the powwow grounds just before Grand Entry,
raced across the field, turquoise and yellow shawls flying,
reached the entrance in time, took our places, smoothed
our hair, and melted into the dance. It was the first gathering
of the season, in April, when the grass is still chartreuse.
To this powwow, called "Celebration of Life," we went
to dance, to give back because we could, and to acknowledge
your death, brother, you who stepped ahead of all of us
and cut your life short by choice. And when the emcee
called for your song, we entered the circle. Hard honor beats
struck elk-hide, the drum reverberating, honoring you, and also
those who remain, in whom the heartbeat struggles against
the desire to die. Warrior-heart brother, we create our relatives
to fit spaces within us. The circle fills with dancers, some crying.
An eagle fan brushes the drum. The bone whistle, held by a veteran,
pierces air—drumbeats pound louder and faster, four repetitions,
dancers giving it all away, dancing you into the next world. We leave
the powwow circle behind, spectators wondering what happened.
Like sunlight between trees, we enter interstices between worlds.
Swirling air affirms our presence. Feathers float down the sky.

II.

"I am telling a story," she said. "It is unfolding as I tell it."

A gathering of wind gods, who cast their game pieces to the ground.
Human bones, teeth. Skin of a bat's wing. Hairs of black-tailed deer.

Whirling darkness.
Whirling darkness.

"It is not simply magic, this work. It has always been made out of words.
And darkness isn't evil," she said. "But it can conceal intention."

The wind gods are known to feel jealousy. Envy. Hatred. Greed.
One of them is laughing. One of them wants everything you have.
Bird-headed god, feathered serpent. Quetzalcoatl, Abraxas.
One of them speaks.

A hallowed word, a curse, an incantation.
Codices. Runes. Scrolls of birchbark. A story that old.
Amulets. Petroglyphs.

        Whirling darkness.

Behind her, hooded eyes of a screech owl.
A promise, untied. Words hang midair.
                                        The utterance,
irreversible. It is happening now.

A heart so immense that when it broke no one could hold it.
It was your heart, brother.

III.

I want my life now in the way of those who have come close to dying.
Soon enough it will be time to travel four rivers whose names have been lost,
            that journey made by those who cross over,
which takes each soul days while our relatives dance us out;
            we travel fighting the current
into whitewater rapids, storms sent by wind spirits who would
like to see us lost,
            toward the last bend, each traveling west in his time,
as I am paddling faster now, already knowing the way—

there, a tulip poplar scored three times by the hatchet, one trained branch
pointing upward, where a solitary Cooper's hawk always sits watching;
there, reeds and cattails that harbor red-winged blackbirds;
a blanket of sedge draping the bank; and now the red medicine elk
picks his way through bear grass, up the incline, unhurried.
His head sways as he works his way toward the bluff
where an Indian emerges from the cedars, bare-chested.
Hair, bound with eagle feathers, streams down his back.
On his chin, the tattooed mark of our people. Quahog shells in his ears.
Each hand grasps a feathered prayer stick, the drum under his arm.

He sets the drum down. Raises his arms. Calls out the sun,
            a glimmer on the edge of the world.
Above him, two eagles are circling.

It is part of the story, not the end or beginning.

Flint and fire. Feathers. The wiping of tears.
Danny. Brother, singing us home.

Weh a hey, ya sa ga oh weh (*ah*)
Ya sa ga, oh weh a hey
Ya sa ga, oh weh a hey . . .

Without Wings

in memory of Mary Belvin Wade

These are only the intricate, ordinary rituals
to which we subject ourselves as women:
rubbing and polishing, mops, copper kettles,
news of your death, stacks of papers, checks,
balanced accounts. We might remember
women laughing, the tribal center kitchen,
a damp spot on the back of a blouse.

It is not the White House, where we
went only once, where gloved hands
in galvanized sinks arranged dainty,
identical hors d'oeuvres on trays. There is no
holy light: only the comforting motions
of scrubbing, and grief, a butterfly outside.
What else? There are no eagles in this poem.

How we go on: the sky a gray, seamless
blank. Then the lake, a white dogwood,
two mockingbirds squabbling. What remains
to be done is everything, daily, again
and again. Some of us will be silenced.
Some will wake less ashamed. Some may rise
without wings to name what injures us.

One in Three or Four

There are too many of us for you
to believe you are either alone or
responsible. No woman asks for
this. Some are children. Some are
boys. Every one of us should have
been heard. This is for Anna, age 17,
who was then beaten and left to die;
for Nathan, who at 11 admired the
basketball coach; for Rosaline, who
sees in her baby the face of a rapist
and who finds that face difficult to
love; for sisters when soldiers came,
mothers imprisoned among guards,
for aunties grandmas daughters sons,
for one who was tied and one who tried
to scream, one whose husband watched,
one violated time after time, one torn
apart, who called the police who
did not call her back, who went to
the clinic where there were no kits,
who numbed her shame with drugs,
who could not drink enough to forget,
who took her life, who believed she
was an object, who said nothing, who
knew no one was there and that no one
would ever be there. Know this: there
are so many that if we could speak,
our voices might spread like floodwaters
over their boots and swell past security
stations; that if we cried out together
we might finally understand it as an
assault on all people, all creation, and
maybe then there would be justice in
this war to claim yourself, a struggle
mapped all over the flesh of every woman
or child who has known what it is to be
used, as you were, your sacred body.

Abracadabra, an Abecedarian

All this time I've been looking for words for certain difficult women
because they aren't able to speak for themselves, and now the
Clinton Foundation has come up with a brilliant campaign—they
decided, for International Women's Day, through digital magic to
erase women on the cover of *Condé Nast*, posters, billboards, those
figures replaced by empty space because women have not yet achieved
gender equity, as noted on a website, not-there.org, and they're right. We
haven't. But when I read about not-there.org and saw its flashy graphics,
I wasn't thinking about how women are not-there-yet, metaphorically, I
just thought about women who are really not there, women and girls who
keep disappearing (not from magazines, who don't make news in Manhattan)
like they've evaporated, like illusions, hundreds in Juárez, twelve hundred
missing and murdered Native women across Canada. The hands of men.

Now you see her. Not. Not-there. Not here, either,

or anywhere. Maybe only part of the problem is the predatory perpetrator-
prestidigitator who more often than not knows her, knows how to keep her
quiet, who may claim to love her, even, maybe getting even—or the serial
rapist-killer in the bushes who bushwhacks her in the dark. You're always safe,
says the forensic psychiatrist, unless a monster happens to show up, and
then you're not. Not-there. Maybe a lonely mandible, maxilla, fibula, or
ulna shows up, or a bagged body gets dragged from the river. Or not. Is this the
value we permit a woman's life to have (or not-have) throughout a wrong
world, a global idea of her as disposable parts? In the end, this is not a
xenophobic poem, not specific—it's everywhere. Not-there. Right here.
Yes, the sun rises anyway, but now the parents are staring past each other, that
zero between them like a chalked outline in their family photograph. Or not.

Deer Woman

He hunted me into the clouds as I sought the blue
star-petaled flower, its scent like magnolia and peach.
I left my family in the meadow to pick my steps
across patched snow, where fields grasped edges of sky.

There is within some of us a longing to be stripped clean.

Alongside, the forest held his shape. His scent rose to me
with the wind. Too late I knew him, too late to find cover,
and I ran as I was made to—haunches taut, nostrils steaming,
like a swallow I darted into glistening whiteness.

When I tired, he was there. His circle tightened.
Dark, and dark-eyed, hypnotic—I could feel his hunger
as my own. I had taunted his dreams more than once,
dreamt that mouth, the merciless craving in him.

There is within some of us a longing to be stripped clean,

to give it all—strings of sinew, tufted hair, marrow,
white ropes of fat, to bare the body's pulse. I froze,
heavy with the need to dissolve into him, his mouth
the deep red song of an appeasable desire.

On the wind I hear another song, my family calling out
to me, calling me into my name. But I cannot return
from this altitude, bound to his hunger, which is a kind
of love. I will kneel in a cloud's wisp of grace, to discover

how completely our own wanting wounds us.

PART II

HEIGHTS

Heights

I.

We stepped through blue air.
As we approached the peak's edge,
your pickup a red blur
at road's fork below, the granite outcrop jutted
like a chin across the county. Below us lay gold threads of rivers,
leaves spinning slowly in descent.

Breathless, we climbed higher, up to the electrical tower,
where you told me about the Great Bear,
three brothers chasing him into the sky,
the way the Bear's blood
marks the leaves every autumn.
Encircled by your arms, I returned
your kiss, the bones of our faces
pressed together hard, as though nothing but love
could exist at that height. You released a ragged leaf,
which seemed never to fall:

something within us wants both
to cling and let go, beyond any terror or longing to fly—
not to plunge, to leap *out*
and be lifted—as though air
could support us, as though we could abandon
our own mortal weight.

II.

Dark against the bank,
I watched your shape rise
from the form of a deer by the creek,
where water caressed round stones.
It might have been last year or five hundred years ago.
You lifted your hand—tobacco to the sky—
a prayer, before your knife
slit the belly and the deer opened, gleaming inside,
guts tumbling, bright blood in splotches on leaves.

You'd spent hours motionless,
waiting for that moment, only that one,
when the doe would come for your arrow—
the way she would turn
to look at you then, as though she knew
how the love in your arms would unfold
and you'd release, muscles unclenching.

III.

The winter was bleached sky,
a gunmetal road, pearled clouds.
Gulls drifted like ashes below scalloped wires,
gray tones against a gray field.
The sun moved—that moment
three apartment windows blazed,
their small fires blooming as I watched
from the restaurant. How we await one particular voice,
unbutton our shirts to it,
daring to love as the clouds coil up—
and then leave together, winds whipping into songs,
to drive south
where small deer graze alongside the interstate
at twilight, like dreams of themselves.

Once I woke in a motel
beside your breath to understand
that our bodies' cells, each lined with glittering dust,
are already disintegrating
like crumbled stars, that generations of lovers
speak through the breeze in the grass.

IV.

But perhaps nothing can be called memory—
are there only collections of cells like our own,
only the grass, stirred by wind?
Or perhaps there is nothing *but* memory,
our bodies called into creation
by histories that recognize us.

And what histories—enough to make love
appear nearly impossible—Opechancanough,
Metacomet, Logan, Cornplanter.
Imagine strangers taking the bodies
of Indian men, their bright knives,
gaudy blood splattered on snow,
hands mounting a head on the palisade's point,
that dark nest of hair where I buried my cheek,
scent of flesh burning   everything
burning. Scalps on the barn wall. Skin separated,
the hacking   the cleaving   the body broken into
again and again, the body   the body   *god*
skin I have haunted,
all those Indian men so like you
and the women who loved them.

V.

When you left me once,
I tried to track your voice
through the spaces it had occupied
between knobby fingers of stair-rail, behind sheetrock—
those measured rectangles of air between the studs,
cobwebbed, smelling faintly of inhabitants who preceded us,
dust obscuring dust, a hundred years since
men raised beams from footers—
all I heard was my heartbeat repeating your steps.

And when you left again, what remained if not memory—
the world shrank to the size of a room,
its walls enclosing all of the past,
my arms, bereft, grasping at emptiness.
Memory—a synapse, a flicker like fire—
the mind twisted over and into itself
until what once was
becomes only a refrain.

I have seen the construction sites where skywalkers work,
the way rows of steel beams jut vertically into the air,
each perpendicular to the one on which you walked,
eight floors up, balanced, as though the sky
had handrails. You were tiny up there,
a bear silhouetted against purpling dusk.
Years ago, you fell forty-five feet,
breaking both legs—you could have died,
of course, but you said
the sky freed you with its silence, and you were not afraid.

VI.

We are dying, this moment,
on our way now toward leaving
each other. The cells will break open
like dark iris buds, and the voice, also broken,
will croak its final utterance
into disintegrating syllables
as it names or obscures what we love.

At night, from the summit, we watched
the valley lights flicker. At night, in a high cave,
dry bones have whispered our names.
We, who have been here nearly
forever, have traced the other's scars—
willing to do *anything* to celebrate this flesh
before saying yes to the dark iris sky,
the night in which enchanted words
swirl like fire sparks above those swollen
roots from which we rose.

PART III

PAST SILENCE

In the Beginning

Ahone, the Great Hare, made the land and the waters, the deer, the fish, and the humans, with the help of the four winds, who came as gods from the edges of the earth. He was afraid to let the humans into the world, because it was a dangerous place, and they were new beings. So he kept them in a bag near the rising sun.

He set the fishes in the waters. He put a Great Deer on the land. But the wind gods grew jealous, and they killed the Deer. Ahone gathered the remaining hairs of the Deer and scattered them over the earth. Then he spoke powerfully and caused each hair to grow into a new deer. There were so many that the winds could not catch them all.

Now the Great Hare thought the humans would be safe. He opened the bag and placed a man and a woman in each country. In this way he brought the world into being.

Sky Woman

Long ago, this world was water without land.
All the people lived in the sky. Some say
a great chief's daughter fell. Others say she
was ill, or that she carried life in her womb.
Somehow she fell from the heavens. Some say she
chased a bear. Some say the tree of life was uprooted
or that people dug it up because someone dreamed it,
and she fell through the hole left behind. Some say
a man kicked her through the hole. They call her
Ataensic, Sky Woman. She fell for a long time.

On the surface, water birds floated. They watched
the woman fall from afar. Some joined together,
so that she could fall onto them. She couldn't swim
like a water bird. They did not know what to do.
The Great Turtle spoke up. "I can carry her,"
he said. She crawled onto his back. Some say
Muskrat dove to the bottom of the world.
Others say it was Frog. Someone swam down
and returned with a handful of mud. Together
they spread it across Turtle's shell to form earth.

Sky Woman gave birth to a daughter, who in turn
bore twin boys. Some say one was good and one
evil. Some say the evil one killed their mother.
One twin made sun, moon, and stars. He made
mountains and trees, new animals, plants.
The other made darkness, storms, dangerous
creatures. When they were finished creating,
the twins fought. Some say one died. Some
say this story is the beginning of everything.
Some say it's not about good or evil but balance.

Bartolomé de las Casas, 1542

So it was that we discovered a flowering island we named "Hispaniola,"
which natives called Haití, or Mountains, and Quisqueya, Mother of Lands.

And the people were guileless, generous, devoid of wicked thought.
They coveted not. They were delicately built, suited poorly for labor.

Into this land of the meek came our Spaniards like ravening beasts,
with methods of torture never heard of before; to such a degree, I believe,

that a number of three million souls is now not exceeding two hundred,
in less than fifty years. Who will believe it? More than thirty islands,

ruined, land pocked in a mad search for gold, people thrown into slavery,
nations destroyed on the mainland; I imagine fifteen million people killed.

Indian men hid children and wives, saying Christians could not have come
from Heaven, and still our Spaniards cut them to pieces, sparing few,

with such abandon that I feared for our souls. Away from laws that govern
civil men, they became worse than brutes; the war dogs were kinder,

for they killed to eat and did not so loudly enjoy it. What of the survivors?
The men died in the mines, women died in the fields, without time

or place to come together. The milk in the women's breasts dried up, infants
perished, and thus was emptied that place which had seemed paradise.

Paquiquineo, 1570

A winged canoe sailed into our bay, with pale-colored men whose faces grew hair upside down. I left with the strangers, wanted to see their world. They called me Paquiquineo. I was the son of a chief, a *werowance*. Who knew ten years would pass before I found my way home?

Ignosce mihi, Pater, quia peccavi.

We sailed to Mexico, where I learned their religion, their talk. Baptized, I became Don Luís de Velasco. I met their king in Madrid, a wondrous place, went to Cuba, saw missions, their craze for gold, the desire of their priests to spread God's word. I would help, I said. In my own land.

Ego te absolvo a peccatis tuis in nomine Patris et Filii et Spiritus Sancti.

We sailed from Havana with Father Segura, Luís de Quiros, six Jesuit brothers, and a boy to lay the mass. We traveled upstream from my village to build their new mission: a church without soldiers, they said. They would call it Ajacán. I found my brother, who offered me leadership, which I no longer wanted. There was a drought, and all were hungry. It was enough to be home.

Ite in pace, ad Deum laudandum et serviendum ei.

They wanted us to feed them, those Jesuits. We had nothing. Priests kept coming, demanding. My brothers grew angry, and I had to choose. My family wanted me. The Jesuits wanted to suffer. We killed them with arrows and clubs, took their robes and the boy. The Spaniards from La Florida came. They killed twenty of us. They wanted me. I was not to be found. We returned the boy, but they captured more men from another tribe. The Spaniards hung them by their necks from the ship's yardarms. A lesson in God's retribution.

Requiem Aeternam dona eis, Domine, et lux perpetuae luceat eis.
Requiescant in pace. Amen.

They never knew my name.

Arrival: Roanoke Island, 1585

> *For a transitory enchanted moment man*
> *must have held his breath in the presence of*
> *this continent.*
> *—F. Scott Fitzgerald*

They call it "The Lost Colony" because people disappeared. English
people, first of them to arrive, who left homes for new lives, who had
that little to lose. Drawn by the slow slap of water against a wood hull,
who knew weeks of scorching sun, squalls, tattered sails, hardtack,
occasional limes to stave scurvy, a queasy seasick scourge. Who saw
perhaps a single albatross, harbinger of nothing, until they sighted land.

Waters, with fish everywhere. Magnificent dunes of the Outer Banks,
shocks of seagrass that spurted through sand. Raucous gulls. Clouds.
Flowers unknown to them. Walls of huge trees, which Frost later called
"the pillared dark." A brave new world. They stared—squinting,
enchanted—breathless, as Fitzgerald said. They were not the only
people in the picture. Others knew this place. They lived there.

Already the leaders were taking stock, figuring. They counted
the ships' masts they saw in those trees, calculated how far
to mountains where they might find gold, imagined saltworks
and industries, plows by the score. That mad tender, their passion
the compulsion to extract. The wondrous moment passed.
They ran out of food. Their governor sailed home for supplies.

Not a ship to be had, for three years. In the colony, the worst drought
in eight centuries lengthened. They did not know how to fish. Deer
watched them starve from the woods. Those who survived lost their minds.
So little remained. Their town, deserted. Only the word "Croatoan"
carved into a tree. Croatoan, Chowanoke—an Indian town just upriver,
where a lion-crest gold signet ring, circa 1580, was discovered.

Later, explorers heard stories. Blonde Indians, living to the north.
Indians who built two-story frame houses, said they learned from
the English. Were the survivors enslaved? Separated? What happened
to Virginia Dare, first English child born in this hemisphere? Somewhere
on the Chowan River, a young Indian woman rocks another child
who gazes at her with gray eyes. They will never be part of the story.

Amonute, 1617

Tsenacomoco. A place like no other, heart of all hearts,
our center, that lime-green breast of a world.
We were of it. Belonged to its waters, which spread west
like fingers from Chesapioke, where saucer-sized oysters
stacked themselves on underwater shelves and shad teemed upriver
when trees budded, such as grew a hundred feet or higher:
cypress, sycamore, chestnut, crowding out the understory. Where,
at forest's edge, white dogwood blossoms shimmered like stars.
Where our women dug *tuckahoe* tubers, pounded out bread, and
planted corn, beans, and pumpkins with songs, according to the moon.

My father, Powhatan, our *mamanatowick*, holiest of chiefs,
who in his dreams entered all realms seeking our futures
                                   and who spoke with our priests the secret holy words,
called me Pokahuntas, little Mischief. A nickname. He knew my name,
Amonute.

Wind from the east, with what portent, the day runners brought word
of more ships with sails, pale strangers with hair on their faces like dogs?
Watch them, Powhatan said. We heard tales: they tried
to catch fish with flat pans, built a wall around their huts.
Could not feed themselves.

Opechancanough, our war chief, captured and brought us their leader.
A squatty short man, face sprouting red fur. No one had seen
such a man or heard his talk. My father exchanged boys with him.
The white boy
would stay in our town. He and I traded words. I learned "house," *yehakin*.
                                   "Bread," *ponap*. "Garment," *matchcore*. "Arrows," *attonce*.
Aroughcun, I taught him, that one with the black-striped tail.
Mockasin, supple buckskin, scent of woodsmoke.

I wanted more words. Went to their fort, to the redheaded man.
Chawnsmit, his name. He became my father's son, called him Father, said
what was his would be ours. I learned to speak to him.
          Ka ka torawincs yowo?
                                                  "What do you call this?"
And my father's question:
          Casacunnakack, peya quagh acquintan vttasantasough?

"In how many days will there come more English ships?"
Then he left. Chawnsmit, our son. We were told he was wounded. He had
died, they said.

That Anglo tongue, my undoing. Years passed.
Oftentimes, we were fighting the strangers.
My husband Kocoum disappeared,
and his Patawomeck people sold me to Captain Argall for a copper kettle.
I was to be ransomed. Was sent to Henricus
where the Reverend Whitaker, a dour man hunched like a buzzard,
instructed me in their words, their religion, and where
John Rolfe came to love me. Our people were at war. Would I marry him,
he asked.
Would my father make peace? We said yes. I gave up my sacred name,
Matoaka, she who kindles,
and I became Rebecca,
a biblical woman who left homeland for Canaan, married Abraham's Isaac,
brought peace between enemies,
bore twins: the red Esau, who emerged first; and Jacob,
who through his mother's treachery inherited the land.

A few years of calm. We planted tobacco. I bore a son, Thomas.
Then another question: would I cross the sea, go to London, be their
emissary?
Yes, my father said. Go. We need to know more.
I saw Plymouth, then London. Felt its crowds press upon me, knew its stench.

I saw that Chawnsmit.
He still lived. No son of ours. Heard their lies in his words.
Knew then that more of them would always come to us.

At last, when spring came and the winds turned, our ship left for home.
I felt weak. I stumbled. We must stop, my husband said.
She is too ill to go on.
He cupped the bones of my face. Wiped my brow when delirium
swallowed me. Spoke gently.
Words.
Black words swirling like London's murmurations of starlings that
clouded the sky at dusk.

At home, my sisters pat out corn cakes and laugh. The elder calls to a child
who splashes at river's edge, where the sand wears each stone smooth.
Crenepo, woman. *Marowanchesso*, boy. *Sukahanna*, water.

On the shore, men scrape dugouts with oyster shells.

Acquintan, canoe.

Words. As though nothing had changed.

It is but the fevered dream of one who sleeps an ocean away.
Tsenacomoco.
We thought it the center of the world.

De-he-wä-mis

(1743–1833)

Born at sea, I have lived between worlds: Ireland
to America, a farm hacked from forest; the family
attacked, captured, marched to Fort Duquesne.
French and Shawnee men dancing, my mother's red
hair on a scalp pole, bright fires.
                                        Two Seneca women
canoed me downriver to a town of longhouses, past
burned heads and body parts mounted on spits. Took me
as sister, gave me a name: De-he-wä-mis, "pretty girl,"
or "pleasant thing."
                    I have tried to be pleasant. Did as I
was asked. Practiced speaking English when alone,
recited my catechism. Named my son Thomas after
the father I'd loved. Buried a husband who fell ill
while hunting, married again, had six more children,
all with English names.
                              Another war, our people
forced to choose sides. Americans burned our towns.
At the Treaty of Big Tree, I spoke to the white men, and
we got better terms.
                    Buried a daughter, my three sons,
my husband. Alcohol. Fighting. Consumption. A landslide.
There were too many whites. Our chiefs chose to leave
for Buffalo Creek. My brother asked if I'd stay or return
to an English-speaking world I'd not known for 40 years.

What would life be among them, how could we belong?
The whites claimed me but not my daughters. Not my Indian
brother, whom I cried for days to lose. I stayed, on my own
land. Told my life to a preacher, who called it a
"captivity story."
                    Sold the land, joined my family. I have not
lived imprisoned; I am not just Mary Jemison now.
At ninety, a woman with choices, I was once made
a relative. Taught to be human. It has been enough.

Black Kettle at Sand Creek, 1864

And the fields? Aren't the fields changed by
what happened?
—Carolyn Forché

red field
        white flag hanging
mountains
        gold sky
creased face
        wrapped braids
nothing lasts long

valley of tipis
        the flag
he cried
        run to the flag
bluecoats
        on horseback
the ridge
        and air
ripping
        ran
and the children
        and screaming

face like etched brass
        bullet holes
silence
        memory immured
a nondescript field
        only the earth
and the mountains

Mochi

a survivor of the Sand Creek massacre

We had to dig holes afterward, in the creek bank, with our hands.
To hide ourselves. We could not feel the wounds. Could not think.

My husband. My mother. Who could describe the noise everywhere?
Children chopped to pieces. Did the soldiers think us human,

stumbling blind through cold to find another Cheyenne camp?
I dreamt a spotted war horse and sang my death song.

Where our people had been, wind like voices. We no longer
inhabited ourselves. Apparitions, nightmares. An unholy fury.

Tsis Tsis Tas. I had no one. Rode with the men to look for that
Chivington, who called himself a man of god. A god who cannot

hear. Then Custer's men came to the Washita. Black Kettle's people
died, as though we could live through it again. Spirit warriors:

we murdered those settlers, kept their children. Surrender meant
nothing. A train to Florida. Leg irons. I was a prisoner of war.

And a woman, once. With shorn hair, I crossed the first of four rivers.
The journey of the departed. I have not been alive, all this time.

Return to San Carlos

(Aravaipa Apache, April 1874)

Because they starved, and the mountains were unknown.

After the massacre, he had come back, she told them.

Children's bones, worn blankets, wind.

As though he might simply live another man's life.

They had slaughtered a horse.

Or as though he could stop feeling love even then.

And could not risk a fire. The meat, raw and tough.

To know she could not have been born someone else.

And at San Carlos, white flour with worms.

Or as though they had decided to go on.

Their men in the sun, making bricks, chained like that.

Years lost to them. Holes in cloth, his breath in her hair.

So many fell sick and died. And an old woman crying.

To say it could have happened differently.

Who could have stood it? They carried their lives on their fingernails, he said.

And she slept in his arms as though he was still there.

Remembering Ira Hayes

born in 1923, the year before American Indians became U.S. citizens
through an act of Congress, without their approval or involvement,
in order to hasten their assimilation

who grew up on the Gila River reservation where Akimel O'Odham people
(known to others as Pima) had lived for more than 2,000 years

who possessed the gift of quiet, his elders might have said, not needing
much conversation

who followed radio reports of the Second World War until in 1942, at the
age of 19, he enlisted in the Marine Corps Reserve for the duration
of what was then called "the National Emergency"

who was trained as a parachutist, nicknamed "Chief Falling Cloud," and
who saw combat in New Guinea

who was stationed at Iwo Jima on February 19, 1945, where he
participated, with one Navy Corpsman and four others from Easy
Company, 2nd Battalion, 28th Marines, in raising an American flag
on Mount Suribachi, the second flag raised that day in one of the
War's final battles, which lasted more than a month, left more than
25,000 American Marines dead or wounded, and almost completely
annihilated the Japanese garrison of 22,000 men

whose flag-raising moment was forever commemorated by a single image
captured by an Associated Press photographer, which won
a Pulitzer Prize, was used to sell war bonds, and became the
biggest-selling U.S. postal stamp of all time, a national symbol of
patriotism that outlived the war, as Ira did

whose buddy Mike Strank, father figure to Ira and the others, was hit a
week after the flag-raising as he guided the company to safety
during heavy sniper fire, the shell tearing his heart from his chest

whose buddy Harlon Block assumed command until a mortar round sliced
him from neck to groin, his intestines dropping to the ground

whose buddy Frank Sousley fell dead from a sniper's bullet several days later during an assault

whose buddy Jack Bradley, the Corpsman, wounded by shrapnel, was airlifted to a hospital in Guam; he later worked as a funeral director, raised a family, and never spoke about the war

who, with Jack Bradley and fellow survivor Rene Gagnon, met President Truman and accompanied the Seventh War Bond tour to 32 U.S. cities

who returned home when the war ended, quieter than ever, plagued by memories of his friends and the fact that Harlon Block had been mistaken in the photo for another man

who hitchhiked 1,300 miles to Block's home in Texas in order to tell his family the truth, and who helped to get the controversy resolved

who noted during ensuing years that strangers would send him cards or simply show up on the reservation wanting to meet him, which made him uncomfortable

who was arrested 52 times for public drunkenness

who like other combat veterans at that time received no help from the military, no way to work through what was then called "shell shock" or "battle fatigue"

who died alone at 32 beside an abandoned shed from effects of alcohol and exposure, less than ten years after the event that made him a national figure, and whose death the coroner termed an "accident"

who received the largest funeral in Arizona history and who was buried at Arlington National Cemetery, which is also the location of a monument that commemorates the flag-raising, the most massive bronze statue in the world at 110 feet and 100 tons; inscribed around its base are the date and location of every major Marine Corps engagement from 1775 to the present, but on it none of the men whose images it depicts are named

who wanted to be a Marine but not a hero.

Apologies

I.

The time has come for the nation to turn
a new page by righting wrongs of the past.

We apologise for laws and policies that inflicted
profound grief, suffering, and loss and for the removal
of children from families, communities, and country.

For the pain of these, their descendants, and for families
left behind, to mothers, fathers, brothers, sisters,
for indignity inflicted on a proud people, we say sorry.

We resolve that the injustices of the past must never,
never happen again and look to a future based on mutual
respect, where all, whatever their origins, are equal partners.

Spoken by Australian Prime Minister Kevin Rudd,
introduced in January and delivered November 29, 2008,
the day after he was sworn into office

II.

I stand before you today to offer an apology
to former students of Indian residential schools

whose objectives assumed that aboriginal cultures
and spiritual beliefs were inferior and unequal.

This policy of assimilation was wrong, caused great
harm, and has no place in our country. Young
children were forcibly removed from their homes.

Many were inadequately fed, clothed, and housed.
Some died. Others never returned home.

Many have told of emotional, physical, and sexual abuse
and neglect, and their separation from powerless families.

To living former students, family members, and communities,
we recognize our wrong in separating children from their cultures.

We apologize for failing to protect you. We ask the forgiveness
of aboriginal peoples for failing them so profoundly.

Spoken by Canadian Prime Minister Stephen Harper
in the House of Commons, June 11, 2008

III.

The United States, acting through Congress, recognizes
years of official depredations, ill-conceived policies,
and the breaking of covenants by the Government;

apologizes to all Native Peoples for the many instances
of violence, maltreatment, and neglect inflicted on them;

urges the President to acknowledge wrongs against
Indian tribes in order to bring healing to this land; and

adds this disclaimer: nothing herein authorizes or supports
any claim or serves as a settlement against the United States.

Introduced by Senator Sam Brownback, then attached to a defense appropriations bill, the U.S. apology resolution was signed in April 2010 and remains undelivered aloud by the president.

What It Is

for Mandy Smoker

Around us, charged
particles of sound:
languages lost, every
word for what matters.

We can feel lightning
before it arrives: the scalp
tingles, sparks course through
capillaries, hairs electrify.

What Indians won't say
in any language: We can't
forgive ourselves because
we lost the land. Lost it.

Does *why* matter? Fenced
out, we turn away but cannot
let go. Every evening, bruised
syllables, trees full of owls.

A cacophony of sirens.
Ghost children, who do not
live long enough to own a past.
Embers smoldering on our lips.

The Weaving

A basket is a song you can see.
—Danny Lopez, Tohono O'Odham (1936–2008)

Where moved   within shadows
what she sought   willow
beargrass   blue lightning
   absence   a color
when she may have wandered

they could not tell her
   colors of fire   amaranth
what can   with words
   where rivers
she braided   or   flashing
black   her color   mountains
and where she sat weaving

coyote   saguaro   moon
fleshtone   tight weft
   or   shape of a star
where wove the color of absence
a shape   and with words
   umber   sepia
formed them   a village
their hands   and the singing

Past Silence

homage to Michel-Rolph Trouillot (1949–2012)

Stories are made of silences. We know this. What matters becomes narrative; what is thought not to matter is excluded. Some call it history, which is one kind of story, with this distinction: in the Western manner, the pretense to exclusive truth. We had other kinds of stories: to show how we came into the world, how to behave—as one among many, to remember holy places that distinguish the land, places touched by spirit—how to avoid mistakes of all kinds, how to find beauty, how to reciprocate, how to think in balance. We knew time as a series of cycles: that we do not progress but repeat. We called ourselves human beings. The People. We were related. We had orators: keepers of wisdom, traditions, faith, law, who were careful not to omit. Who gave us the stories in winter, when animals were silent and we gathered near our fires. It was a good system. It worked well for thousands of years.

We

The unthinkable happened. Disaster. Which defied definition. Defied even the words with which our questions were phrased. We had no instruments for imagining this. Others entered our world. They named things that had names. Created fields of power. Semantic, transformative power. They named us. The silences began when they "discovered" us, when we became Other. Homeland became wilderness; land virgin (read: *empty*). Inhabited land. They could own it. Doctrine of Discovery. They could take it. Degrees of humanity. We were now not quite human. Our past appeared in museums of natural history, with dinosaurs, insects, and rocks. Not in history museums, with stories of human beings. The illusion of dichotomy; *i.e.*, history begins when they arrive, is preceded by pre-history. Thousands of years of pre-history, excluded. Because they were not here. *Ipso facto*. Palimpsest: the covering of an ancient text by writing over it. In archaeology, the burial of a site by building on top of it. Call it the Americas.

We are

"Is it really inconsequential that the history of America is being written in the same world where few little *boys* want to be Indians?" How do we recognize a bottomless silence? We became invisible. Passive voice: no one was responsible. Words were manipulated. Words like *extinct. Disappeared. Vanished.* Mists of history obscuring the gaze. Words like *authentic. Full-blood.* No real Indians remained. A language of euphemism: discovery, not conquest. Battles, not massacres. Language of simplification: villages, not towns. Gardens, not agriculture. Survival skills, not science. Legends or myths, but not history. Language of interpretation. Words like *savage.* Like *lore.* Past tense. Lived in tipis. Hunted buffalo. Wore feathers. Like *dead.* We began to believe this story. Became imprisoned in invisibility. Because it did not matter whether we fought or surrendered. Words like *culture.* Like *traditional.* The bottomless argument: Who is an Indian? We became self-destructive.

We are still

And all the commemorations. Four or five hundred years of this or that. Others decide what is momentous and why, as though their imagined destiny foreshadowed the sequence of events. Archival power. Retrospective significance. Primary sources. Marching bands, Knights of Columbus, Plymouth Rock, Santo what's-his-name. Packaged history. Pocahontas, Thanksgiving: American myths for public consumption. Heritage tourism: What is it worth? Who wrote this story? Who imposed silence on neglected events, filled that silence with new stories (read: *about power*)? How they invented democracy, free enterprise, cultural plurality. As though these did not already exist. As though it was a New World.

We are still here

The past is not history. It is all of what happened, not some of what some have said happened. Truth lies not in being faithful to a view of what mattered but in confronting the present as it re-presents the past. In examining current injustices. We create and recreate the past in the present. Only then can we participate. Revise narratives, insert absent voices. Seek words that resist erasure.

PART IV

THE NAMING

The Naming

Some nights we feel the furred darkness
of an ancient one's breath and are trapped
in awakening, dismembered
by events we no longer recall.
We can touch the windowsill,
where October air gathers
as hours slip past in thin robes,
the forest a concert of voices.
The last crickets let go of their songs.

The land speaks, its language arising
from its own geography—
the mountains' hulked shapes
are blue whales, remembering
when they were undersea ridges,
and rivers are serpentine strands
hammered from silver, and dark trees
talk to the wind—weaving mortal lives,
drumbeats, pillars of smoke,
voices wavering into updraft,
the storyteller shifting the present.

*****

Imagine another arrangement of stars.
Beneath them a man, so old he has never
not been among us, raises his rattle-stick,
palms the bone nuggets, gnarled roots,
earth's incantations, and he speaks
from behind the hunter moon
your first language, your name.
As he calls you from a maelstrom,
he imagines you, molded from words.
Through love you begin,
and something condenses—
through utterance you come into being.

*****

Tuned for utterance, our senses
are like gates encircled by landscapes
of voices—antlers and feather shafts,
rivers and cliffs that have spoken to us.
We exchange possibilities
with forms, textures, bright webs
of meaning inhaled through the skin.
The sky's hue and rushing of waves
talk to us and within us.

Imagine a black lake
reflecting constellations, a river of light
and, between earth and sky,
fireflies pulsating, mirrored
in water, like three worlds of stars.

Receive the night's density.
Enter its water—
that grace, which allows us to sleep.

*****

When we locate the sleeping bear's den,
we cannot speak of it aloud, because
the bear's spirit will hear. Women call it
hulzinh, meaning "black place,"
where bear spirits once spoke their laws.

In the autumn, when bears have grown fat,
we travel with dogsleds to the dens.
If we point at a bear we have seen,
it will vanish. So we speak to it: "I am
your friend—go slowly—put up your head."

Neggenaa eenlaanh, noolaaletl'onh.

The bear gives its life as a gift,
and we make its ceremony as for one of our own.
We consume the bear's life.

We walk for the bear in the Koyukon way.

When we find him, he offers himself.

*****

With our tongues we offered
names to the waters that still
speak of us: Shenandoah, Mississippi,
Iowa. Minnesota, Niagara,
Illinois. Will our enemy's children
hear the rivers singing those names?

Among our stories it is told
how a chief led survivors
of his people across a great river.
Striking his stake upon the dry ground,
he exclaimed, "Alabama!"

Here we may rest.

*****

Names have determined the world.
To use them, call language out whole,
immersing yourself in its sounds.
We are made from words, stories,
infinite chances through which
we imagine ourselves. Estranging
ourselves from the sensual world
in which language was born, we will die.

What if, as through history, a language
dies out, if its names cannot be uttered
or if they exist mapped
as place markers no one interprets:
Passapatanzy, Chattanooga, Saratoga?
They are part of the ground,
a language of vanishing symbols.

*****

Is this what we are now,
fragmented,
a language of shattered dispersal?

Grief keeps watch
across a field darker than water.
We live in a wounded space,
voiceless cries breaking with all
utterance, even the idea of utterance.

Without a vocabulary, how
does the story continue? in words
that have murdered the people
before us, their voices airborne
like corn pollen, out into the desert?

*****

In the Akimel O'Odham desert,
we celebrate the songs of ants and orioles,
given to dreamsingers in a distant time.

Through hundreds of poems,
each a rendering of dream,
we are calling the singers
of past generations. They come forth
among us now—ancestors, beings
of sky and of earth—through the dance
and the dreams we connect.

ne'e *ne'e*

Our songs reflect occasion
through a poetry of sequence.

If you think that birds and insects
cannot dream, you are not listening.
Around us—from the air
and from the field—
ants and orioles come singing.

*****

When we walk for the peyote, what we know
changes shape and shifts meaning,
for nothing can be as it was.
The symbols we take with us—
gourd bowls, yarn discs, and arrows.
When everything is made, we pray,
we set out, and the meanings
must change to unite everything.

The *mara'akame* tells the seekers
his dream, and the dream changes names
every year. That which is sacred
reverses. Call the women flowers.
A man's clothes become fur,
doves become eagles, a cat a coyote.
We will hunt the sacred deer, calling them
lambs. Everything must be right.

Tévi *Uká*
Chíki *Táu* *Mecéri*

When we cross over to another country,
we turn the world backwards to hunt
the peyote, which is alive. We return,
make a ceremony, and the names change.
Our world grows familiar again.

*****

The world is an open field
reciprocating us, living pulses
of streambeds dried into grass,
mountains with cheekflesh exposed,
winds that echo the elk's mating cry.
What precedes our knowing—
this collective landscape
of which knowledge always speaks?
Can you know the sequoia
without caressing its bark?
When you touch it, it also touches you.
You have walked through its forest of eyes.
Land whispers a geography—

when you live in a place long enough,
it will recognize you, as your body
of membranes exchanges itself with the air.
You are not above the land but within it,
rooted in soil, related with all that completes you.
Are the rocks dead? They merge,
they were once shards of boulders,
they will turn into dust as we will.
In the end we begin in the depths of the earth.

*****

Into the earth, they went away to hide.
When their destroyers rode in, the air shattered—
gold plains were strewn with bodies
left to rot, skinned humps of marbled meat
humming with decay. When the earth
cradled their skulls like white crocus bulbs,
they went into the ground.
They could not return until we sang to them.

Tatanka Oyate ku pi
Tatanka Oyate na-unx'un pi

Do you remember when we lived as people
who prayed when they offered themselves?
Now they stand fenced with guardrails,
hooves mucking the earth.
No one sings when they die.
Someone keeps saying, "Aren't they just wonderful?"
Look at them. Ask their forgiveness.

*****

Can we forgive our grandfathers
for leaving the bones of their relatives
to the wolves?
Their voices grow thin on the air.
We can hardly hear them now,
their cries not those of warriors but children,
voices lost mourning injuries,
the vast desolation of the people.
These are graves scattered about,
and a wailing soughs through the tall pines.
Only ashes remain.

The warriors have gone to the west,
but here lie the dead.

Nunahi duna dlo hilu-i

Now they are shadows, scarcely reaching
our knees. The people are scattered
and gone. When they shout, they can hear
a sound deep in the forest, but nothing
comes back. And now their words are few.

*****

In the forest, beyond the village palisade,
one hut crouches like a boulder.
The holy man works to balance
forces of wind, animals, insects,
rivers, stones, each with its language.
From here he listens and journeys entranced
into realms no one inhabits.

Now he rises from kneeling by the fire,
takes the rattle from its hook,
lifts his arms to the moon.
His voice is thin smoke, blue corn
popping, a coyote over the ridge.
He would speak, we might say.
As the river speaks, and sometimes we hear it,
its story a song of the water's beginning.

*****

It goes on, through its water,
an accounting of reminders,
not legends, of cloth strips
and implements left along a road.
It goes on through a voice
speaking names and events.
Somewhere a family plods west,
their backs hunched with belongings,
weighted by what they carry
or a home they will not see again.
Their descendants ride
eastward, retracing their steps.
Somewhere the faces of children
at Sand Creek and Carlisle,
the various mappings of war.
Somewhere the calls of wolves echo.

*****

Now the wind lifts a circling
dust, and all that has been
begins rising—ancestors'
chipped flints and potsherds,
photographs, cartridge shells,
acorns and jerky, buffalo dung,
cavalry uniforms, medals from
Washington, antlers, arrow shafts,
blankets, bones, discarded tires,
shattered glass, ashes in fire pits,
dry-rotted baskets, tobacco ties,
tin cans, commodity wrappers,
Indian names and the names
strung before us, cavern walls
painted with white petroglyphs,
pressed forms of insects and fish
gone to rock, and the rocks
to air swirling, settling again
into the silence we become.

ACKNOWLEDGMENTS

I thank the editors of the following publications, in which these poems first appeared, often in earlier versions:

American Indian Culture and Research Journal: "Sky Woman"
Four Winds: "Red Elk"
Fulcrum: An Anthology of Poetry and Aesthetics: "The Weaving"
The Kenyon Review: "The Naming"
Native Innovation: American Indian Poetry in the 21st Century: "Mochi"
Red Ink: "One in Three or Four," "Triolet for the Road"
Rendezvous: The Humanities in Montana: "Homeland"
Shenandoah: "Deer Woman," "Return to San Carlos"
Sing: Poetry from the Indigenous Americas: "To Keep Faith"
South Atlantic Review: "Bartolomé de las Casas," "Paquiquineo," "Arrival: Roanoke Island, 1585," "What It Is," "Past Silence"
Studies in American Indian Literatures: "Amonute, 1617," "De-he-wä-mis"
Tough Times Companion: "Dancing the Stars," "Without Wings"
Yellow Medicine Review: "Apologies," "Black Kettle at Sand Creek, 1864," "Remembering Ira Hayes," "The Egg."

I'm grateful to Adrienne Brown, Carolyn Cades, Janet McAdams, and Kevin McFadden for insightful comments and suggestions; to numerous students at George Mason University's writing program for review of some of the poems; to Carolyn Forché fifteen years ago; to Allison Hedge Coke, Deborah Miranda, Tara Causey, Poets House in New York, the International Poetry Festival staff and volunteers in Medellín and Bucaramanga, Colombia—Luís Rendón especially—and many unnamed friends.

NOTES

The epigraph is by Czesław Miłosz, from *Bells in Winter* (Ecco Press, 1974, p. 5).

"One in Three or Four": In the U.S., one in three American Indian women has experienced rape or attempted rape (*New York Times*, May 22, 2012, citing Justice Department figures). One in four girls and one in six boys will be sexually assaulted by the age of eighteen (National Crime Victimization Survey, Bureau of Justice Statistics, U.S. Department of Justice, 2000).

"In the Beginning": This is the origin story of the Powhatan people, related by Iopassus (Patawomeck) to Captain Samuel Argall, 1610.

"Sky Woman": This is the creation story of Haudenosaunee (Iroquois) and Huron peoples, which has many variations.

"Bartolomé de las Casas": las Casas, a priest, participated in Columbus's second voyage and the Spaniards' cruelties toward Indians. He became an *encomendero*, owning Indian slaves. Witnessing the conquest of Cuba, he grew convinced of the immoral nature of the colonial enterprise and renounced his landholdings, freeing his slaves. He argued persuasively to Spanish authorities for more humane treatment of Indians, spending fifty years of his life as a religious activist. His efforts improved the legal status of slaves but failed for the most part to change the ways in which they were treated. His "Brief Account of the Devastation of the Indies" (1542) is a graphic indictment of the conquistadors' encounters with indigenous peoples.

"Paquiquineo": The Latin lines, from the Catholic Mass and Last Rites, translate as follows:

> *Bless me, Father, for I have sinned.*
> *I absolve you of your sins in the name of the Father, Son, and Holy Ghost.*
> *Go in peace, to praise and serve God.*
> *Eternal rest grant unto them, O Lord, and let perpetual light shine upon them. May they rest in peace. Amen.*

"Arrival: Roanoke Island, 1585": The epigraph is from F. Scott Fitzgerald, *The Great Gatsby* (Charles Scribner's Sons, 1925). Robert Frost's line, "the pillared dark," is from his poem "Come In."

"Amonute, 1617": For contemporary interpretations of Pocahontas's life, see Camilla Townsend, *Pocahontas and the Powhatan Dilemma* (Hill and Wang [Farrar, Straus and Giroux], 2004); and Helen Rountree, *Pocahontas, Powhatan, Opechancanough: Three Indian Lives Changed by Jamestown* (University of Virginia Press, 2005). For the Powhatan word list, see *A Vocabulary of Powhatan* (American Language Reprints, vol. 4, Evolution Publishing and Manufacturing, 1997).

"De-he-wä-mis": For sources on this autobiography, see Isabel Ayrault, "The True Story of Mary Jemison" (in Edward R. Foreman, Rochester Historical Society Publications Fund Series, 1929, Rochester Historical Society 8: 193–218); and James Seaver, *A Narrative of the Life of Mrs. Mary Jemison* (New York: American Scenic and Historical Preservation Society, 1824 [1942 edition]).

"Mochi": Mochi was among the first officially documented female U.S. prisoners of war. She survived Colonel (Reverend) Chivington's horrific massacre of unarmed Cheyenne at Sand Creek, Colorado, in 1864 and became a warrior. With her second husband, Medicine Water, she raided white settlements for more than ten years. They surrendered at Fort Reno, were imprisoned without trial, and were eventually transported to Fort Marion in St. Augustine, Florida. Released in 1878, Mochi and her husband returned to their people, who had been forcibly moved to Oklahoma. She died among them at age thirty-seven.

"Return to San Carlos": San Carlos is an Indian reservation in Arizona where several Apache tribes were confined under brutal health and environmental conditions in the early 1870s. Those who left the reservation were hunted down by U.S. soldiers and frequently killed as "hostiles."

"Remembering Ira Hayes": For a rendition of Hayes's story, see Arlington National Cemetery's web page at www.arlingtoncemetery.net/irahayes.htm and also *Flags of Our Fathers*, by James Bradley, son of Jack Bradley, who was at Iwo Jima (Bantam, 2000). The book became a major motion picture.

"What It Is": This poem is a response to M. L. Smoker's poem "Equilibrium" (in *Sing: Poetry from the Indigenous Americas*, ed. Allison Hedge Coke, University of Arizona Press, 2011). Line 17 is a quotation, used with the author's permission.

"Past Silence": This manifesto was inspired by Michel-Rolph Trouillot, *Silencing the Past: Power and the Production of History* (Beacon Press, 1995).

"The Naming": I am indebted to the following sources that focus on indigenous peoples' uses of languages, historical accounts, or meditations on communicating about atrocity:

David Abram, for the image of three worlds of stars and the concept of perceptive reciprocity (*The Spell of the Sensuous: Perception and Language in a More-than-Human World*, Vintage, 2007 [Introduction]).

Richard K. Nelson, for a report on bear hunting among the Koyukon people (*Make Prayers to the Raven: A Koyukon View of the Northern Forest*, University of Chicago Press, 1983).

Donald Bahr, Lloyd Paul, and Vincent Joseph, for accounts of traditional song-poems among the Akimel O'Odham featuring ants and orioles (*Ants and Orioles: Showing the Art of Pima Poetry*, University of Utah Press, 1997).

Ramón Medina Silva, for a discussion on how language is reworked to accommodate the sacred during peyote gathering ("How the Names Are Changed on the Peyote Journey," in *Imagining Language: An Anthology*, ed. Jed Rasula and Steve McCaffery, MIT Press, 2001).

Maurice Blanchot, for ideas on the unutterable regarding horrific experiences of history (*The Writing of the Disaster*, University of Nebraska Press, 1995).

Leslie Marmon Silko, for sharing an indigenous perspective on the nature of stones ("The Pueblo Migration Stories," in *Speaking for the Generations: Native Writers on Writing*, ed. Simon Ortiz, University of Arizona Press, 1997).

T. C. McLuhan, for collecting the speeches and stories of American Indian leaders (ed., *Touch the Earth: A Self-Portrait of Indian Existence*, Promontory Press, 1971). See speeches of Eagle Wing; Colonel Cobb (Choctaw Chief); Young Chief (Cayuse) at Walla Walla, 1855.

Ludwig Wittgenstein, for views regarding conceptual confusions surrounding language use, including semantics (*Philosophical Investigations* [1953], John Wiley and Sons, 2009).

ABOUT THE AUTHOR

KARENNE WOOD is an enrolled member of the Monacan Indian Nation. She holds a PhD in linguistic anthropology from the University of Virginia and a MFA in poetry from George Mason University. She directs Virginia Indian Programs at the Virginia Foundation for the Humanities. She has worked as the repatriation director for the Association on American Indian Affairs and as a researcher at the National Museum of the American Indian. Wood held a gubernatorial appointment as Chair of the Virginia Council on Indians from 2004 to 2008, and she has been honored as one of Virginia's Women in History.

Wood's first book of poetry, *Markings on Earth*, won the North American Native Authors' First Book Award. In 2002, she was selected as Writer of the Year in Poetry by the Wordcraft Circle of Native Writers. Her poems have appeared in *The Kenyon Review*, *Orion*, *Shenandoah*, and in numerous other journals and anthologies. This is her second collection of poems.